SHORT STORIES
FOR BUSY LEADERS

Inspire Future Generations

Written by
KEITH MARTINO

ISBN-13: 978-0-9791669-8-3

ISBN-10: 0-9791669-8-5

Also by Keith Martino

EXPECT Leadership - The Executive Edition

Leadership Guides
EXPECT Leadership in Business
EXPECT Leadership in Engineering
EXPECT Leadership in Technology

Sales Handbooks
Get Results
Results Now

This book is dedicated to the memory of my friend, James William Goode and to our Most Gracious and Loving Heavenly Father.

January 8, 2019

Short Stories for Busy Leaders

Table of Contents

Introduction...

I wondered why James was always smiling.

I'd see him at church, in the community or running school board meetings. It was always the same. James smiled continuously and contagiously. He smiled at chamber events. He smiled at business luncheons. And he smiled when he engaged you one on one.

I was in the audience one evening when the Master of Ceremonies unexpectedly veered off the program to recognize James. He called James out as an example of one of their city's finest leaders. James simply smiled.

One recent Sunday afternoon in the midst of a long car ride, I pressed for an answer, and James gladly shared his secret.

"The secret is to find the nugget and pass it on."

He said, "Keith, life is just a series of stories connected one by one. And each story has a purpose... a golden nugget that can be learned and shared with others. The secret is to find the nugget and pass it on."

Suddenly, I understood. James smiles because he is mining for the golden nugget in every adventure... good or bad, happy or sad. James finds a reason to smile.

And when the school board elections finally stopped going his way after decades of dedicated service, James was right there the next day in our Sunday morning class. They asked him to lead the opening prayer and I must admit, I sort of cringed inside. James smiled!

Then he bowed his head and led a prayer of gratitude far beyond any prayer I could have imagined. He thanked his Creator for a lifetime of blessings.

Knowing James makes me happy—through the jolts, jars and injustices of life. And I'm learning to smile more often. I'll listen for the story. Search for the nugget. And try to brighten someone else's day. Just like James.

1

Think Like An Owner— And One Day You Will Be

Jerry wasn't your average engineer.

While his college classmates fascinated on academics, Jerry raced down the sidelines snagging sizzling passes for the Baylor Bears. Soon he scored a much sought after intern offer from NASA and bought an acoustic guitar to serenade the boot scooters.

What could have been more thrilling than to see an inspired young man from Shreveport, LA reaching for the stars and achieving success? But, ultimately talent is finite, youth is fleeting and good looks are quite common.

Expect to Succeed

As Jerry rose through the corporate ranks, the traits that made him his company's most valuable player year after year had little to do with his athletic prowess or his love for a catchy tune. Jerry's secret formula was his priceless perspective. His worldview.

Jerry thought like a business leader. Every day. In every situation. And when the opportunity presented itself, Jerry overcame all the challenges of an economically distressed childhood to buy majority ownership in his company. Jerry thought like an owner and became one.

Could you do the same? Could you propel yourself into another universe by changing the way you approach your job? We believe you can. We hope you will. But, hope is not a strategy.

As it turns out, there is no average engineer. There are only engineers who think like employees and engineers who think "like a boss." The daily choices you make are indicative of the path you're on. So test yourself while there's time to adjust and ramp up your game.

Expect to Succeed

Do you expect to succeed? Here are twelve questions you can quietly ask yourself to predict your outcome.

True or False:

_____ I do what is right for my customer, company, and team regardless of personal sacrifice.

_____ I press forward with good ideas, even if they are unpopular.

_____ I aim for goals higher than any manager will set for me.

_____ I do not give in to group pressures simply to avoid confrontation.

_____ I consistently give truthful feedback to customers, superiors, and teammates.

_____ I adhere firmly to a code of business ethics and moral values.

_____ I believe change always brings opportunity. Stagnation limits opportunity.

Expect to Succeed

_____ I practice a disciplined approach to self-improvement.

_____ I have a method for prioritizing my opportunities today.

_____ I successfully make others enthusiastic about opportunities that require extra effort.

_____ I transmit a sense of purpose about all that I do.

_____ I am accountable for my actions and accept responsibility for my mistakes.

If you answered true to nine or more of these statements, you are on the right road to wind up steering your own endeavor. If you answered false to three or more of these statements, you'll likely always report to someone else. It's all a matter of your objectives.

Expect to Succeed

Jerry knew from early in life that he wanted to reach his full potential, whatever that might be. I have no doubt that if you asked him today, he'd tell you that he's still in the relentless pursuit of excellence. In other words, he isn't done! He's still streaking for the goal line.

Baylor University recently built a stunning new stadium in Waco, TX with world-class amenities. On any given Saturday night, you'll find Jerry up in the stands. His heart is always in the game.

And if you wander up to Jerry, ask him if you should aspire to own your own company. He will likely chuckle, wish you much success and suggest that you will have to make that decision for yourself.

But regardless of your goals, Jerry will say, "be the best YOU that you can be!"

. . . . .

"Think Like An Owner – And One Day You Will Be" was featured in **Hot Wires**, musings by the electronics design industry's best minds.

2

Profits or Politics? Where's Your Company's Focus?

On paper, Bryce was a rock star. In person, Bryce was a costly mistake.

When Bryce strolled through his company's headquarters sipping his gourmet triple latte and waving to the little people (as he dubbed them), every front line employee noticed. They snickered at his confident strut leftover from his days fronting a band.

They recognized his disdain for real work. And they were appalled by his self-serving power plays. Sure, Bryce flashed plenty of smiles. He slapped high fives and offered up empty promises like a candidate running for mayor.

Promote
Productive
People

But poor follow-through was Bryce's legacy. He seldom kept his word. In short, Bryce was a leadership disaster!

How does one spot an emerging "Bryce" before his decisions crater your company?

Here are five ways to detect a political player like Bryce in the making.

1. Corporate politicians fixate on irrelevant numbers.

Take our buddy Bryce for instance. Bryce kept "real-time stats" on the total number of employees who reported into his organization. Bryce frequently boasted that a significant portion of the operation reported to him or one of his people. That's how Bryce boosted his shaky self-esteem.

He added people while he talked a great game and tried hard not to mess up in front of his boss. Bryce figured as long as he had an adequate number of people to throw under the bus at the opportune moment, he would be too big to fail. Bryce fixated on employee count, not profitability.

Promote
Productive
People

2. Political players recruit, hire and promote bureaucrats like themselves.

It's true. Birds of a feather flock together. Self-absorbed power junkies are obsessed with protecting their titles at all costs. Consequently they try to hire people who are singularly loyal to them.

Often they find themselves at odds with an underling more loyal to the company. When they do, they will quickly take any measure imaginable to rid their team of those who are looking out for the good of the whole.

Fortunately, oil and water don't mix. Employees and leaders who are truly concerned about the welfare of the company are turned off by those who seek to play the system.

Case in point: Bryce's demise began when his peer-level executives became as disillusioned with him as his front line employees were.

Promote
Productive
People

Bryce's hiring and promoting of other politically minded employees initially went unchecked because his colleagues were immersed in their own immediate concerns.

3. Political players cover up.

After all, the Bryces of the world tend to perform for an audience of one. Their boss!

Political players will often freely (and unnecessarily) sacrifice their team's welfare for the sake of keeping the boss happy or shielded from the truth. This is not always a reflection on their boss.

He or she may have been misled about the details two or three levels down. Political players like vagueness and fuzzy business practice. Transparency is not typically a hallmark of their character.

They operate in the shadows where almost no one has insight to their treatment of the people. They love "weasel wording"!

Promote Productive People

4. **Political players encourage a zero sum mentality.**

Some got to win, some got to lose. That's the chorus to every song for a corporate politician. In their world, there is no such thing as a win-win outcome. And their department heads also propagate this win-lose mindset.

The political player seldom takes the time to seriously evaluate a balanced option. They want to win at all cost. And their politically-motivated direct reports know instinctively not to cross the boss. It wouldn't be prudent.

Political players win by short-changing the organization.

5. **Political players come with plenty of hidden costs.**

As I later met with the CEO's management team, we inventoried the true cost of having Bryce in power. It became apparent that he had made dozens of unnecessarily costly decisions.

Promote
Productive
People

Bryce built a division that could never reach profitability. He pushed technology that he preferred versus exploring for new IT solutions that would best serve the company. Bryce delegated all authority to managers who were either asleep at the switch or pandered for his favor.

As a result, the company was paying extraordinary sums for expensive logistics initiatives that delivered a poor customer experience. Bryce's salary and benefits were only a tiny fraction of his real cost to the company.

Sooner or later the results speak for themselves. The results of Bryce's self aggrandizing moves were draining the company's balance sheet and delaying success. Once realized, Bryce was given a fair severance package and hustled out the door.

Avoid the heartache, headache and howling that political players bring to their companies. Hire and promote only those people who combine character with competence.

Promote
Productive
People

Ask yourself these five questions about each member of your management team:

1. Does _____ fixate on irrelevant numbers?

2. Does _____ overlook or ignore loyal company employees who do good work?

3. Does _____ recruit, hire and promote individuals who pander to them?

4. Does _____ quickly adopt the easy solution that best serves their self-interest?

5. Does _____ make costly decisions because s/he is self-absorbed?

If any of your leaders (or employees for that matter) cause you to answer "yes" to three or more statements, you have an opportunity to lower your operating cost substantially.

Consider replacing that person with a competent leader who really cares about your company. If you must, look outside your company. Remember... hire for character and train for skills.

Promote
Productive
People

Ironically, Bryce's follow-up gig gave him the spotlight to swagger like an actual rock star. You can catch Bryce and his new band playing weekends on the Jersey Shore. At least now the only cost for watching Bryce perform is the cover charge.

Don't put a political player on your payroll. Promote productive people!

Today is the day to shine the spotlight on each of your company leaders and objectively evaluate their performance.

. . . . .

"Profits or Politics?" was featured in *Construction Business Owner Magazine.*

3

Encourage Your Team With One Word

The lights sparkle in Debbie's eyes.

She is fired up and ready to launch into our closing exercise of the leadership discussion. Our finale is an experiment destined for success. How could we be so certain? Easy. We'd seen it work wonders on many occasions including with Debbie's group a day earlier.

Debbie's second group is more famished for encouragement than the first! It is comprised of corporate executives and systems professionals under heavy pressures and tight timelines.

Cultivate Camaraderie

These leaders carry the responsibilities of managing departments and organizing the company for the future.

It is now the end of their company's fiscal year. They are spent. Energy levels are understandably taxed. Tensions simmer.

Debbie's approach is the game changer. She is a strategic chess master. Her goal is clear. She wants to send each person back out into their rough and tumble world with a smile on their face and a spring in their step. And she wants them to feel better about themselves.

You might be curious why Debbie would be so fascinated with lightening the emotional load in a work group where technological demands typically dominate the discussion.

After all, much of the dialogue of the day is focused on wireless networks, scheduling applications and handheld mobile scanners. The systems are humming. Even on days when her people are dog tired, Debbie is building winners. It's her leadership style!

Cultivate
Camaraderie

We've found battle fatigue to be the case in many technology teams over the past decade. With all of the drama, illness and animosity bubbling over in our contemporary landscape, many people are simply shell shocked and weatherworn by adversity.

They can handle the complex systems challenges. But the people problems are becoming like rocks in their shoes.

So how can you bring renewed energy into your group with a fresh and simple activity? Here it is. It's called the "one word" game! Want to play?

1) Ask your technology group if they are absolutely prepared to be honest with their colleagues around the table.

Gain closure that each person will speak only the truth as they reach out to the peers in the game. No exaggerations! Establishing this commitment is essential.

Cultivate Camaraderie

2) Provide each team member with a list of the names of the people in the room. Ask them to write "just one word" beside each name that accurately describes each person in the most positive and accurate way they can envision. Words like "honest", "sincere" and "methodical" are just a few examples of adjectives that cultivate camaraderie.

3) Ask each person to stand and deliver a truthful compliment to each of their peers. For instance, Lauren might say to Sean, "Hi Sean, I believe that you are ENTHUSIASTIC." Sean simultaneously keeps a running list of all the positive, truthful compliments delivered to him.

4) After the game concludes, each person stands and reads their list of personal adjectives provided by their teammates using statements like, "Hello, I'm Sean and I am "Enthusiastic," "Entertaining," "Inspiring." Applaud after each person shares their list of personalized, positive attributes.

Cultivate Camaraderie

5) After they've finished, ask the group these three simple questions:

   a. How many of you feel better about our company after hearing these words?

   b. How many of you feel better about this team after hearing these encouraging words?

   c. How many of you feel better about yourself after hearing this encouragement?

Allow a few minutes for them to thank one another for the kind words shared and send them back out into the workplace. You'll be amazed at the results.

The lights sparkled in Debbie's eyes.

She was fired up and ready to launch into our closing exercise of the leadership discussion. Our finale was an experiment destined for success. How could we be so certain?

Five words this time...
Try it! You'll like it!

. . . . .

"Encourage Your Team with One Word" was featured in *Women in Technology International* magazine.

CHAPTER

· · · · ·

4

Why Corporate Dysfunction Is Deadly

Matt took great delight in our mentioning that his sales team was effectively dysfunctional. He praised their competitive, "take no prisoners" mentality. He beamed each time a winner taunted a struggling teammate. He stoked the notion of "beat your brother's brains out."

In short, Matt rationalized how this fierce, aggressive, individual pursuit of success was healthy within a world class sales organization.

It worked. Matt's branch shot to the top. Profitability soared. Banter replaced camaraderie.

Nurture Teamwork

And true to their word, senior management promoted Matt amidst great fanfare. After all, Matt was their rising star. He knew how to "get results!"

The crash took a year to incubate. Matt's promotion gave him national influence and responsibility. And with the informal mindset of "every man for himself," Matt's new branches stopped sharing best practices. They lost sight of their common objectives. They relished this new "do your own thing" mantra and embraced it with zest.

Soon production managers picked up on the insular mentality and it spread. They created their own metrics and over-hyped the rivalries. Marketing joined the fray and Matt raced the company rapidly over a cliff.

Matt's termination was announced quietly. Today he's looking for a job.

So, is internal competition a bad thing? Of course not. But once friendly competition replaces collaboration as the corporate culture, it wrecks companies, teams and lives.

Nurture Teamwork

Is ruthless competition the only form of divisional dysfunction?

Nope. What about departmental arrogance? Or how about passive aggressive mischief? What about sloppy execution or the failure to meet deadlines?

What about favoritism or inter-departmental isolation? These are all symptoms of a lethal "me" versus "we" mindset.

Here are three reasons you should eradicate dysfunction ASAP.

- The best employees want to be successful in something larger than themselves.

- An individual's lack of consideration for a peer yields animosity between departments.

- It's hard to foster unity of spirit unless everyone is contributing daily to the momentum.

Nurture Teamwork

How do you know if your company is showing the strain of dysfunctional behavior?

1. When you walk through the office do you see plenty of smiling faces?

2. Are team meetings energetic and productive?

3. Are your departments meeting or beating collective deadlines?

4. Are your most talented new employees voluntarily helping your company recruit new teammates?

5. Are you exceeding your goals for customer satisfaction and financial performance?

We would maintain that if your answer is "no" for two or more of these questions, you are subtly or visibly suffering from some level of dysfunction in your company.

Nurture
Teamwork

Matt took great delight in our mentioning that his sales team was effectively dysfunctional. He thought superstars took ultimate satisfaction in personal victories. Matt turned his head when "winners" were unkind to their teammates. And he did little to light the flame of the team torch.

An old comic strip called Smokey the Bear promoted the slogan "Only you can prevent forest fires!" Start today. Nurture teamwork. Before there's a raging blaze.

Your company's future will be bright when you carefully and consistently snuff out the dysfunction.

. . . . .

"Why Corporate Dysfunction is Deadly" was featured in **Women in Technology International** magazine.

5

Exec by Day, Firefighter by Night

Eddie scaled the catwalk, looked back and heard a loud boom.

Out of nowhere, chemicals exploded. Workers scattered. Smoke clouded the first floor. And faster than a sow chews corn the blazing facility lit up the sleeping neighborhood. Local fire professionals trembled at the probability of a second and larger blast.

It was a bleak picture. Most folks panicked. Some shed tears.

Fight
Fires
Fast!

Joe calmly sipped coffee two townships away. He had already put in a full day's work. Serving his community that evening as their Volunteer Fire Chief, Joe diligently scanned his first responder radio for any sign of distress. Nothing showed in his immediate vicinity. But Joe instantly recognized the address of a rapidly burning building miles away. It was home to his corporate office.

Joe gave the signal and his unit sprang into action. When they arrived on the chaotic scene, Joe's counterpart, a locally paid Fire Chief, promptly tossed in the towel. He shook his head and mumbled his regrets.

His unit had decided to let the massive building burn to the ground. "It's too late. The risk is too high," he rationalized. Joe was stunned, but not deterred. Joe's group offered to step up and take over. The first Chief sighed with relief and handed Joe the reins.

Joe's team brought high octane intensity and passion to the fight. Simply put—they cared! They cared enough to put every ounce of energy into making a difference.

Fight
Fires
Fast!

Joe's crew brought a higher purpose to the firefight. It wasn't for the dollars. Joe fought for the cause.

They fought hard on behalf of the 300 families who depended on this long time employer for a paycheck. Joe himself had invested almost a decade working for this world class roofing manufacturer. He wasn't about to watch his dreams and his peers' future go up in smoke. Joe had not yet begun to fight.

As you know, not every leader runs towards the flames.

Some leaders run from every smoking object they see. They spot a looming disaster and hightail it for the hills before they are singed. Or they quickly look for someone else to blame. Sometimes they duck their heads and pretend not to notice. Others ignite the torch. Not Joe.

Joe's Legacy: Apply Courage, Judgment and Intellectual Stimulation!

Fight
Fires
Fast!

Joe brought a different style of leadership to bear. He was a motivated steward with a steel resolve and an unrelenting passion to solve the problem. Instinctively, he interjected courage, judgment and intellectual stimulation into his steady stream of proactive communication. It was his legacy. Leaders fight fires fast! They refuse to dawdle.

#1 - Courage is an essential character trait for an extraordinary leader. Real leaders are not afraid to take a stand regardless of the prevailing political winds.

They view each dilemma (large or small) as a challenge that can be overcome. And when others wave the white flag in premature defeat, they pick up the banner and charge the hill.

Sure, there usually is personal risk involved when they verbalize a strong position. Courageous leaders balance the cost versus the potential rewards and take decisive action. Like Joe did.

Fight
Fires
Fast!

#2 - Judgment is also crucial. While the first Fire Chief arrived at the premature conclusion that the building itself wasn't worth saving, he never considered the livelihoods and dependent households represented therein. He simply looked at the aged building and assumed it was not worth his unit's efforts to stop the raging fire.

Furthermore, the first Chief never asked questions. He had no idea where the stockpile of chemicals was stored in the factory. He could have sought insight from Joe who knew the landscape well. Instead, he was quite willing to hand off the responsibility at his first and most opportune moment.

When the fire was ultimately extinguished by Joe's squad there was minimal damage. Of course it later became an embarrassment that the home town team had bailed out so early.

Great leaders get the facts, weigh the options and make the right decisions even when they are inconvenient. Courageous leaders exercise sound judgment and motivate their staff to think outside the box.

Fight
Fires
Fast!

#3 - Intellectual stimulation is the ability to get peers to think about old problems in new ways. Joe encouraged his guys with intellectually stimulating queries. He challenged his guys to find more rapid and direct ways to extinguish the flames. Joe's approach identified and eliminated the ineffective fire fighting methodologies employed by the first unit on the site.

As usual, Joe's guys loved the challenge of finding new ways to reposition each piece of their gear. They refined action items through the lens of clear-eyed judgment.

Then they implemented a courageous solution that soon brought this escalating nightmare to a halt. No one was injured. The building was saved.

I saw Joe the Chief Operating Officer and Volunteer Fire Chief recently. He wasn't fighting a building fire. He was waist deep in his day job and had just de-escalated another hazardous event. This one potentially threatened his direct reports at work.

Fight
Fires
Fast!

As a student of great leaders, I had to ask Joe's subordinates how Joe had handled the emergency situation. No surprise here! It was another classic story for their corporate history books.

Once again, Joe calmly and courageously stepped forward in the midst of a costly error made by co-workers. He demonstrated clear judgment by surveying the situation to see if anyone was hurt. He never placed blame. He took charge and challenged his team to put together a creative plan to ensure it never happened again.

Are you an executive and a firefighter in your company? Apply courage, judgment and intellectual stimulation!

. . . . .

"Exec by Day, Firefighter by Night" was featured in **Young Upstarts** magazine.

6

A Sincere Apology Saves the Day!

"How do YOU apologize?"

The question came from the least likely suspect in the crowd. Bob, a former LAPD detective was now a seasoned IT leader for a global retailer. He had seen it all and Bob had the scars to prove it. He was truly perplexed by my off-handed suggestion. I had mentioned it so casually. "If you let someone down, apologize."

I thought his surprise inquiry was a joke. But Bob wasn't smiling. Neither were his peers.

Right
Your
Wrongs

At first I chuckled, then scanned the conference room for a hidden camera. I soon realized the detective had instinctively turned over the biggest clue of the day. This was a large IT organization smoldering in distrust, resentment and frustration.

Bob wasn't finished. "Can we practice apologizing?" "Sure," I responded with a lingering tinge of disbelief. This surprise detour wasn't on our agenda.

Bob looked directly at a fellow executive and said, "Phil, I'd like to start with you." Phil was stunned. The tension between them was legendary. I couldn't believe what I'd inadvertently triggered. And that's when Bob fumbled the ball.

"Phil, I… I… I… guess I owe you an a… a… a…pology" he stuttered uncomfortably. Instinctively, I pointed out to Bob that this was merely a statement of fact—not an apology. Bob tried again and again until he had looked Phil in the eyes and expressed the healing words most needed. Phil couldn't wait to return Bob's genuine gesture.

Right
Your
Wrongs

Their sudden transparency set off a domino effect. Incredibly, we spent the afternoon with every member of the senior staff voluntarily stepping up and apologizing to one another.

They apologized for missed deadlines, caustic remarks and ego crushing power plays. It was riveting to see these grown men and women wiping back the tears as their peers humbly apologized for intentional and accidental blunders.

I left the session that afternoon scratching my head. Obviously, a force greater than me had been at work. Furthermore, Bob's initial apology ultimately saved that team from total implosion. When I returned to their corporate headquarters a month later, the smiles and warm collaboration were still going strong.

So what's the point? If you sense dysfunctional behavior between individuals or departments, act NOW!

Dysfunction is deadly to companies, teams, individuals and families.

Right
Your
Wrongs

Here are three proven steps to repair toxic relationships.

1) Politely raise the issue and challenge the people involved to set aside the past.

2) Demonstrate how to correctly apologize to others by selecting someone to whom you owe an apology. Sincerely apologize as they observe your actions.

3) Gain a commitment from your team that when they let others down in the future, they will respectfully apologize immediately.

"How do you apologize?"

- Look in the mirror and ask yourself to whom you owe an apology.

- Create a quiet encounter where you can look that person in the eyes and say, "I truly apologize for..." Be specific. Be clear. Be sincere. Right your wrongs.

- Then commit to do your best in the future to never repeat that mistake.

Right
Your
Wrongs

Over the years, we've helped unravel varieties of corporate dysfunction. Typically the more technical the team, the more frequent the number of personality clashes.

You don't need to be lead detective on the Los Angeles Police force to spot a dastardly dysfunction robbing your team of success, unity and good vibes. The day Bob learned to apologize his life got better. So did his leadership with colleagues, family and friends.

And when people are at odds, a sincere apology often saves the day! Right?

. . . . .

"A Sincere Apology Saves the Day!" was featured in the **Women in Technology International** monthly magazine.

7

Taming the Multicultural Butterfly

We were almost set for the session to begin.

Wu arrived early. Xiao came late. And Big Mike sauntered in with a nasty disposition.

Vijay came eager to help. Gorbachev tiptoed in anticipating drama. And JT scooped up a couple more donuts and hunkered down to catch the show. Other employees scrambled around, and the room soon filled to capacity.

It was the most unlikely assortment of colleagues I could envision. An international crowd with a true Texas cowboy twist.

Diversify
to
Unify

Jimmy Chow, the shrewd senior exec sat quietly watching it all unfold. His patient demeanor beamed optimism.

Out of the blue, things turned ugly. Big Mike launched into a rant highlighting the intolerable differences between Chinese and Americans. His condescending tone raised eyebrows. Tempers flared.

I gulped twice and wondered if it might take a miracle to transform this group into a cohesive, high performance team. Jimmy Chow never said a word. He sat quietly watching things develop.

So what can you do when your team members find more reasons to clash than to collaborate? It's easy to overreact. It's also tempting to ignore their conflict. Neither is the perfect solution. But what's the right balance?

Act decisively. While storms can blow over, there is a severe risk in sticking your head in the sand and avoiding the drama.

Diversify
to
Unify

A cultural misunderstanding can torpedo your team, destroy any unity and corrupt all communications. As a leader, your actions matter! I knew it wasn't an option to let Big Mike's caustic remarks go unchecked. The gathering clouds were ominous.

So I invited Mike to join me in the deserted hallway. He was stunned. I explained the need for him to demonstrate his best leadership.

He didn't seem [or want] to understand, so I spelled it out again. This time with a bit more passion.

Imagine Mike's chagrin when I emphasized that we needed him to help reset a new and more positive tone for the multicultural group. I asked him to become a galvanizing influence on the team.

I wasn't sure what to expect as we stepped back into the conference center. He wasn't a happy camper.

Diversify
to
Unify

So what can you do when your team is comprised of people who are like butterflies of many colors and don't partner well?

Our recommendation: Find the common ground. Establish an agreeable set of guiding principles that apply in all instances. Stay the course and steadfastly cast everyone's eyes on the team objectives. Never flinch.

Embrace a cross-cultural environment that reinforces "this is our workplace for the present and future." Now is the time to diversify to unify.

In this case, Jimmy's corporate objective was to create a unique "work-smart culture." This would give his company a competitive edge in his marketplace. This became our collective mantra. We refocused the group and simultaneously built a human connection between the people.

Here's how: We applied three specific team building exercises. They work wonders for bringing together a diverse crowd.

Diversify
to
Unify

- **Exercise 1** - Show your group how to encourage their teammates.

- **Exercise 2** - Teach your employees how to apologize when they let a teammate down.

- **Exercise 3** - Coach your team how to thank others for their help and support.

These suggestions may sound basic, but fundamental interpersonal skills are no longer commonly practiced in many companies.

Many leaders have sidestepped their leadership responsibilities in favor of managing the herd with stats and ultimatums. Accountability is essential. But as leaders we are relying upon mere mortals who are constantly experiencing the ups and downs of our contemporary times.

They need the moral support of their peers. We all do. To ignore this fact is unrealistic and shortsighted.

Further compounding the matter many employees in today's diverse workforce have

Diversify
to
Unify

been deeply scarred by not being valued in the workplace.

As our society has shifted gears from the industrial age to the high tech era, the component left behind was the human element. We somehow stopped being nice. But it's not too late.

People around the world are starving for the human touch. Hence, you will find a special opportunity in the multicultural workplace to build an exceptional team.

Make no mistake, there's great value and power in saying "I'm sorry" and "thank you" in the corporate world.

The first time someone sincerely apologizes or says a genuine "thank you," the entire work environment shifts.

The fiber of these comments fortifies the bonds between employees. And when these skills become habits they also establish profoundly important building blocks in the multi-ethnic company.

Diversify
to
Unify

Big Mike made an even bigger turnaround and contribution that day. By the time we finished with our session that summer afternoon, the team had settled down and recommitted to the principles they aspired to reflect.

Surprisingly, Mike apologized for his behavior to his boss and to the Chinese Americans sitting beside him.

As leaders, it's up to us to set the framework for our team. Let's not forget that they too are people with fears, hopes and dreams. And as Jimmy Chow demonstrated, we need to show patience. Our patience shapes who we become as leaders.

As mentioned, Vijay came eager to help. He shared some words of encouragement to the team at the end of the session that revealed his pride in being part of this larger endeavor.

Jimmy Chow sat quietly watching it all unfold. His patience and optimism were rewarded!

Diversify
to
Unify

Show your group how to encourage their teammates. Teach your employees how to apologize when they let a teammate down. Coach your team how to thank others for their help and support.

You can tame the multicultural butterfly. Leverage diversity to create unity!

. . . . .

"Taming the Multicultural Butterfly" was featured in **Commercial Construction and Renovation** magazine.

8

Have You Experienced Millennial Magic?

I'll admit I was a tough sell.

I'd seen and heard many promises about how great life was going to become once I turned over control to young colleagues. I've been told they will work out AMAZINGLY well. I've been led to believe the results would be AWESOME!

I've even been advised that certain people were RIDICULOUSLY talented... whatever that means. When they let me down, I was the first to shriek, "I told you so!"

Engage and Empower

I always considered "old school" to be a compliment and assumed that these Kool-Aid hawkers were in cahoots for favors from the next generation.

But lately, I've been of a different persuasion.

I've experienced first hand that one plus one can equal five when the right folks get their hands on the wheel.

And once they take you for a breathtaking spin into a mind-blowing sunset, it's much easier to toss them the keys again and again.

How would you define Millennial Magic?

My definition as a business owner is simple. Millennial Magic is that unexpected moment when a person puts our business interests first, ahead of their own agenda and delivers excellent results far beyond anything I could have imagined or replicated.

Engage
and
Empower

Typically, they achieve these results without constant supervision or significant direction. And when they present their deliverables to me with a sense of well deserved pride and humility, I'm humbled, too. I call that "Millennial Magic."

Lately, it's been happening more and more often. Perhaps, it's because I've become more open minded about the probability for these events to occur. But I'd also like to think that we've stumbled upon some ways to spark this creativity and imagination in the hearts and minds of younger employees.

Here are three examples of Millennial Magic that I've witnessed recently:

Ashley has always been a reliable and trustworthy team member. Yet, there were many occasions when I avoided taking chances on her improvisational personality. I deemed the stakes were too high in our company.

After all, I've been at this for a long time, I rationalized. Besides, I have a set way to conduct interviews and record the responses of potential alliance partners.

Engage
and
Empower

Ashley on the other hand took an audio file from one of our recent interviews and turned it into an excellent showcase of how we might better spotlight our capabilities for clients.

Her vision for how cloud based technology could enhance our communication efforts produced a high-quality tool that I never would have envisioned.

And Ashley did it quickly, without much need for intervention and with remarkable charm. Her perspective was the leverage she applied that I could never have anticipated or expected. Her vision and technical acumen made it a reality.

Example two: Brian was a talented young professional with much unrealized potential.

His biggest hang-up was a fear of committing himself to a particular role in his company. He felt he had lots of interests and was concerned this would limit his potential to grow and learn.

Engage
and
Empower

After several attempts by his boss to woo him into roles that were in his view too restrictive, she changed tact and offered him some options to simply lead various projects. In other words, she got Brian into the right seat on the bus.

Brian's collaborative nature manifested itself immediately.

Soon one large project that had been delayed several times began to take shape. Cross-functional employees throughout the manufacturing concern became interested in contributing their discretionary effort to make the project work.

Brian adapted his timetable to capitalize on the momentum generated by his colleagues. The project rapidly got back on schedule and turned out to be quite strategic for the future of his company.

Brian is now leading a mission critical distribution arm and his direct reports are engaged and energized. Brian's Millennial Magic is spreading like wildfire.

Engage
and
Empower

Then there's Ruth, a young lady with a solid, trustworthy name and a spectacularly vivid imagination. Ruth doesn't wait for her boss to come to her with assignments. She's always two steps ahead and has found more resources for her company than her leaders can cultivate.

Ruth has found new clients for her firm. She has uncovered referral sources who have delivered new clients. She has established a substantial database and continues to mine it for opportunities daily.

And just when you think Ruth is done for the day, she pulls another rabbit out of the hat that could potentially double the size of her company.

Ruth is too young to technically qualify as a Millennial, but we won't tell her. She's magical too!

If you're still waiting to taste the fruit of the up and coming generations, here are five bold suggestions to improve your probability for success:

Engage
and
Empower

- Take a significant company initiative and describe the desired results clearly without prescribing the methodology for completion. Be specific about outcomes and the timeline.

- Forget titles. Offer it up as a "pilot opportunity" to the young professional you believe has the greatest passion and ability to accomplish the goal. Passion is key.

- Allow the person or people who most desire the opportunity to determine the tools, resources and teammates they would like to leverage to accomplish their goals.

- Ask for three updates per week. Use each feedback session to applaud the progress and reemphasize milestones. Avoid hovering.

- Applaud all meaningful collaboration by fellow teammates and reward successful progress at every measurable moment. This will engage and empower creativity at every level.

Engage
and
Empower

You will know within two weeks or less if the project is gaining traction. If you are seeing signs of tangible success, celebrate the wins and ask what you can do to help.

If the project is languishing or begins to stall out, suggest other resources or discontinue the initiative.

Most importantly, win, lose or draw... ask the person or team to explain to their colleagues what they set as an ultimate goal. Have them describe the approach they chose. Ask them to share the results and lessons learned with the group.

And finally, celebrate the success of the outcome or learning experience!

It's taken most companies a little time and a few false starts to figure out how to best optimize the working relationships between baby boomers and the generations that follow them.

Engage
and
Empower

The great news is that we are seeing exponential evidence of the Millennial Magic.

Don't settle for an illusion! It's real.

. . . . .

"Millennial Magic" was featured in ***Young Upstarts*** magazine.

In Closing...

James was a story teller. He was a leader. And he was a man who freely offered up his valuable golden nuggets. So can you!

As you race through the rigors of this world fighting fires and speeding toward success, remember the men and women who have provided stories you can build upon.

. . . . .

You and your team will:

- Expect to succeed

- Promote productive people

- Cultivate camaraderie

- Nurture teamwork

- Fight fires fast

- Right your wrongs

- Diversify to unify

- Engage and empower future generations

Keith Martino's leadership strategies and articles can be found in business publications including:

- *American Express Open Magazine*
- *Arizona Business Magazine*
- *Builder Magazine*
- *Central NY Business Journal*
- *Circuits Assembly Magazine*
- *Commercial Construction and Renovation Magazine*
- *Construction Business Owner Magazine*
- *Custom Home Magazine*
- *Elevating EAP Awareness Online*
- *Entrepreneur Magazine*
- *FedEx Manager's Pak - Worldwide Edition*
- *For Construction Pros.com*
- *Hot Wires Magazine*
- *Institute of Industrial and Systems Engineers Monthly*
- *Las Vegas Business Press*
- *LinkedIn – The Leadership Perspective*
- *News Times Magazine*
- *NewsMax Magazine*
- *Progress in Lending News*
- *Red Latina Worldwide*
- *Remodeling Magazine*
- *Trucking News Online*
- *Women in Technology International News*
- *Young Upstarts Online Magazine*

Visit www.KeithMartino.com

Acknowledgements

As we close this book, I can't help but remember all of the friends, family and exceptional people who inspired ideas and stories to make this book possible.

First, "thank you" to those who showed the patience to mentor me along the way. I will never underestimate the power of their positive influence.

Bill Brookes, Brad Beldon, Chip Harper,
David Cottrell, Debbie Tripod, Dickie Deising,
Don Rodgers, Dr. Peter Drucker,
Dr. Raymond Taylor, Dr. Thomas J. Stanley,
Ed Bonneau, Ed White, Eddy Ketchersid,
Frederick W. Smith, Glyn (Buck) Gore,
Greg Hext, James Goode, Jerry Smith,
John Dealey, Joseph Olivere, Julie Kelly,
Lane Cubstead, Lou Holtz, Luke Allmon,
Max Lucado, Melvin Gwinn, Michael Beldon,
Michael T. Glenn, Rob Lowe,
Robert S. Thompson, Ron Shinault,
Ruth Martino, Steve Sunwall, Todd Miller,
Valentine Martino, Waldon Gwinn, and last, but certainly not least Wallace Moorehand.

Acknowledgements
Continued...

And I'd like to thank five gentlemen who model quiet leadership daily. See if you can spot their rock solid characters in the stories.

Brian Murray, Eddie Irrizary, Jerry Smith, Jimmy Chiang, and Fearless Joe Tripod. They rock!

Please offer a salute to our Editor in Chief ... the one and only Lane Cubstead. If you find a stray comma or an extra hyphen, Lane can make it disappear or use it to bring value. Your choice!

And then there is the special chorus of lovely ladies who make me want to sing every time I'm with them—Olivia, Laura and Melody Martino. I love them dearly.

A super special shout out to the one person who makes my life and every book complete, my soul mate for over four delightful decades, Terri Martino.

And finally, most of all... to God be the glory. Great things He has done!